IF I MET AN ICE AGE ANIMAL

IF I PLAYED BASEBALL WITH DODO BIRDS

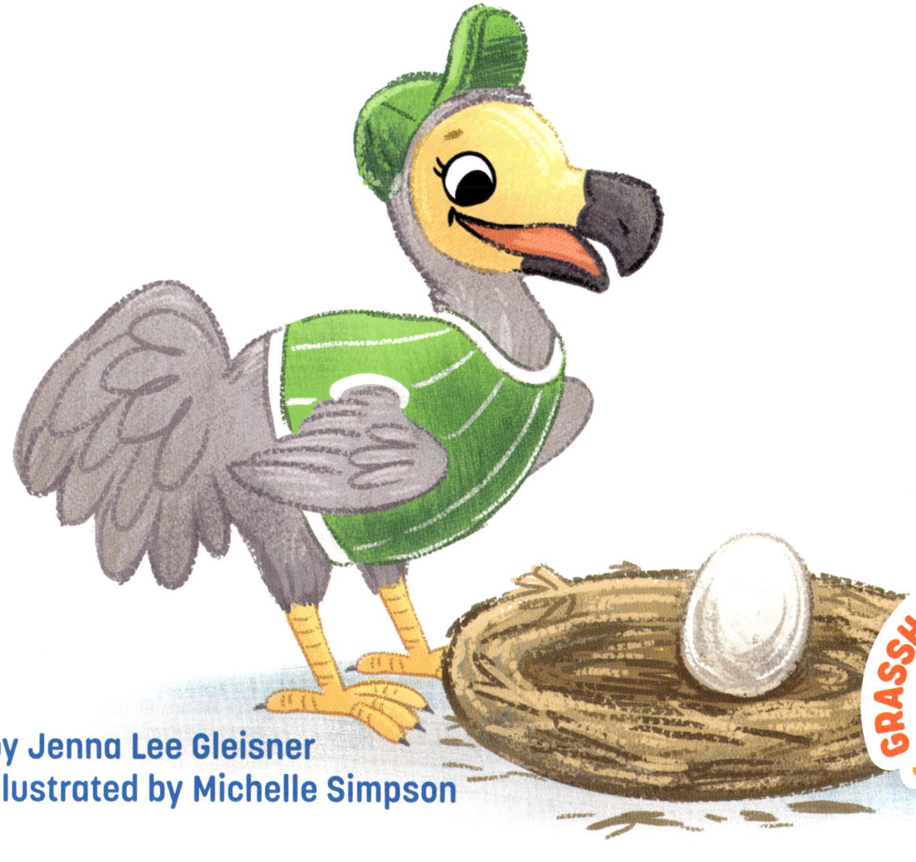

by Jenna Lee Gleisner
illustrated by Michelle Simpson

Tools for Parents & Teachers

Grasshopper Books enhance imagination and introduce the earliest readers to fiction with fun storylines and illustrations. The easy-to-read text supports early reading experiences with repetitive sentence patterns and sight words.

Before Reading
- Discuss the cover illustration. What do readers see?
- Look at the picture glossary together. Discuss the words.

Read the Book
- Read the book to the child, or have him or her read independently.
- "Walk" through the book and look at the illustrations. Who is the main character? What is happening in the story?

After Reading
- Prompt the child to think more. Ask: The main character imagines playing baseball with dodo birds. If you could play a sport with any animal, what would it be? Why?

Grasshopper Books are published by Jump!
5357 Penn Avenue South
Minneapolis, MN 55419
www.jumplibrary.com

Copyright © 2023 Jump! International copyright reserved in all countries. No part of this book may be reproduced in any form without written permission from the publisher.

Library of Congress Cataloging-in-Publication Data

Names: Gleisner, Jenna Lee, author.
Simpson, Michelle (Illustrator), illustrator.
Title: If I played baseball with dodo birds / by Jenna Lee Gleisner; illustrated by Michelle Simpson.
Description: Minneapolis, MN: Jump!, Inc., 2023.
Series: If I met an Ice Age animal | Includes index.
Audience: Ages 5-8.
Identifiers: LCCN 2021060746 (print)
LCCN 2021060747 (ebook)
ISBN 9781636909455 (hardcover)
ISBN 9781636909462 (paperback)
ISBN 9781636909479 (ebook)
Subjects: CYAC: Dodo–Fiction. | Birds–Fiction.
LCGFT: Picture books.
Classification: LCC PZ7.1.G5885 Ifh 2023 (print)
LCC PZ7.1.G5885 (ebook) | DDC [E]–dc23
LC record available at https://lccn.loc.gov/2021060746
LC ebook record available at https://lccn.loc.gov/2021060747

Editor: Eliza Leahy
Direction and Layout: Anna Peterson
Illustrator: Michelle Simpson

Printed in the United States of America at Corporate Graphics in North Mankato, Minnesota.

Table of Contents

Bases and Birds	4
Parts of a Dodo Bird	22
Picture Glossary	23
Index	24
To Learn More	24

Bases and Birds

Today, I'm playing baseball.
My team is playing the Dodos.

What if I played baseball with real dodo birds? I wonder.

If I played baseball with dodos, I'd have to fly to Mauritius. This island is the only place they lived. Before the Ice Age, it was warm.

But during the Ice Age, it was covered in ice and snow. If I played baseball with dodos, I'd have to wear winter gear. Dodos had feathers to keep them warm.

The dodos could clear the bases. They could brush the snow off with their tail feathers.

If I played baseball with dodos, I'd throw the first pitch.

Dodos couldn't fly. But they ran fast! Number 4 spreads his wings. It helps him balance.

If I played baseball with dodos, the whole flock would watch. They wouldn't need stands. Why? They sit and nest on the ground. Mothers each keep one egg warm.

If I played baseball with dodos, I wouldn't have to bring my own peanuts. Dodos find nuts and seeds to eat.

I wouldn't have to open them either! Dodos use their bills. *CRACK!*

Just then, I hear another *CRACK!*

I catch the ball!

That's silly, I realize. *Dodos can't play baseball. And they are extinct!*

Parts of a Dodo Bird

Dodos weighed around 50 pounds (23 kilograms). They were about three feet (0.9 meters) tall. Take a look at the parts of a dodo.

Picture Glossary

balance
To keep from tottering.

bunts
Taps a baseball lightly with a bat so that the ball doesn't go very far.

extinct
No longer found alive and known about only through fossils or history.

flock
A group of dodo birds.

Ice Age
A period of time, about 10,000 years ago, when a large part of Earth was covered with ice.

Mauritius
An island country located in the Indian Ocean, off the eastern coast of Africa.

Index

bases 10
bills 19
bunts 13
egg 16
feathers 8, 10
flock 16
fly 6, 14
ice 8
Ice Age 6, 8

Mauritius 6
nest 16
nuts 18
pitch 12
ran 14
seeds 18
snow 8, 10
wings 14
winter gear 8

To Learn More

Finding more information is as easy as 1, 2, 3.

❶ Go to www.factsurfer.com
❷ Enter "**ifIplayedbaseballwithdodobirds**" into the search box.
❸ Choose your book to see a list of websites.